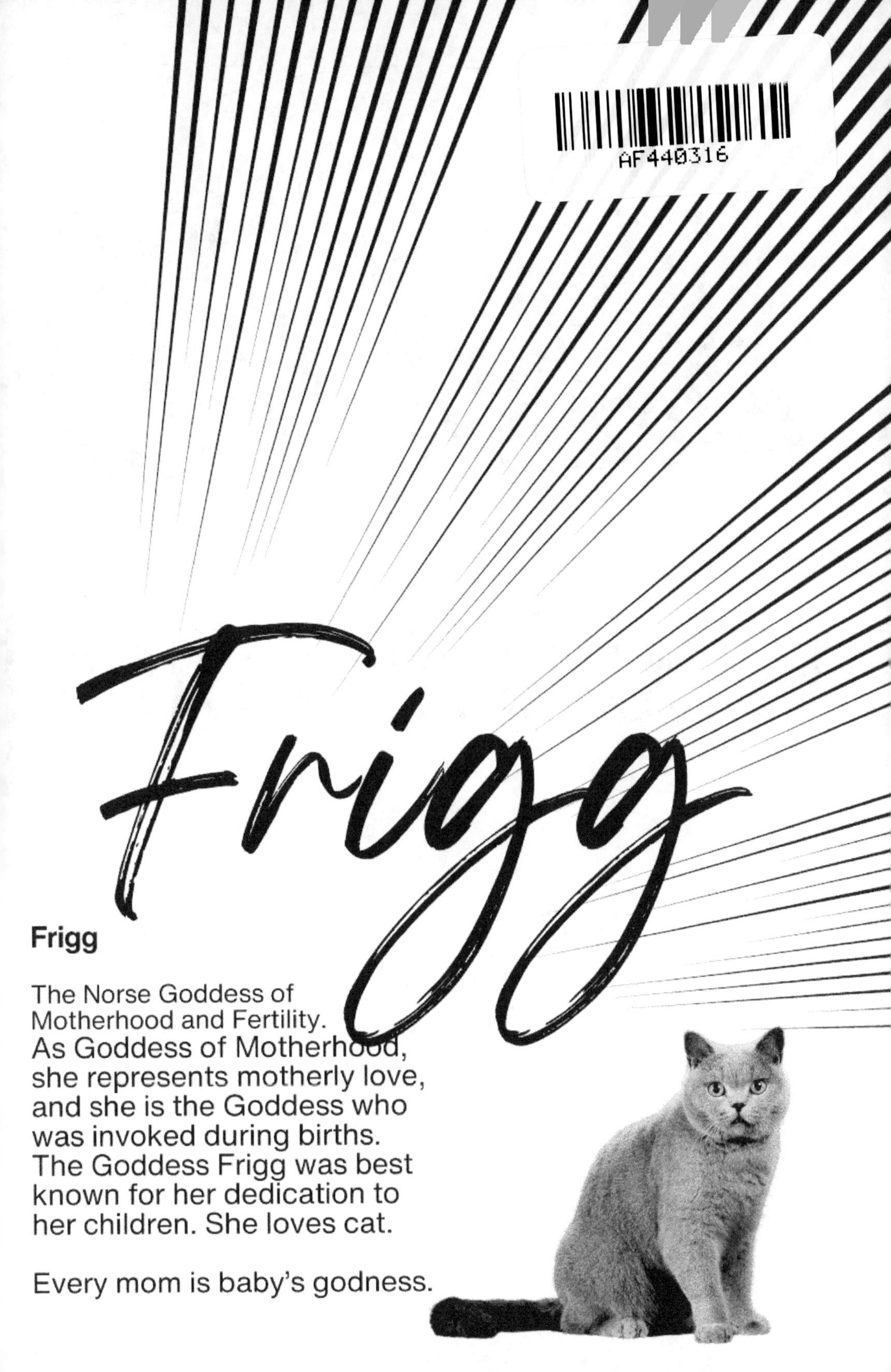

Frigg

Frigg

The Norse Goddess of
Motherhood and Fertility.
As Goddess of Motherhood,
she represents motherly love,
and she is the Goddess who
was invoked during births.
The Goddess Frigg was best
known for her dedication to
her children. She loves cat.

Every mom is baby's godness.

Viporia & Votext

My boys' furry pals, Viporia the white lady hamster and Votext the dapper black dude hamster, have been the dynamic duo of joy and friendship in our home!

WHY
1250 Nights

FROM PREGNANT TO 3 YEARS' OLD, ABOUT 1250 DAYS

WHY 1250 DAYS IMPORTANT?

Pumping resources into tiny tots aged 0-3 turbocharges their brainpower, supercharging their language, motor, emotional, and social skills for a future bursting with success and joy! Especially during the AI Era.

**THE BIGGEST SECRET
IS YOUR MIND.
OPEN IT.**

FRIGG'S 1250 NIGHT STORIES

JOANNA LIU

BioAi Thinktank Press

Table of Contents

INTRODUCTION

Dear Parents and Caregivers,

Welcome to "Frigg's 1250 Nights," a unique educational journey designed to guide young minds through the complexities of growing up in the AI age. This book is crafted to support the crucial developmental period from pregnancy to age three—approximately 1250 days—recognized as the cornerstone for a child's lifelong growth.

Meet our protagonists:

Frigg: A wise and nurturing British Shorthair cat, embodying the challenges and joys of modern parenthood. As a single mother balancing a career with family life, Frigg navigates the pressures of work, societal expectations, and the ever-evolving landscape of technology.

Frigg is s wise and nurturing British cat living in Kensington London with her Daughter Viporia and Son Votex

Viporia: Frigg's daughter, a curious and sometimes stubborn kitten whose insatiable quest for knowledge drives much of the family's learning adventures. Her frequent "But why, Mom?" questions serve as a catalyst for exploration and discovery.

Votex: Frigg's son, a bundle of energy and mischief whose playful antics often lead to unexpected learning opportunities. His enthusiasm for life brings joy and sometimes chaos to the family's daily routines.

Through nightly stories and daily adventures, this book addresses key themes:

1. Balancing technology use with traditional learning and play

2. Nurturing curiosity and critical thinking skills

3. Understanding and navigating the emotional challenges of growth

4. Exploring the ethical implications of AI and emerging technologies

5. Fostering strong family bonds in a digital world

Each chapter is carefully structured to provide:

- A summary for parents, outlining key learning objectives

- Engaging narratives that bring complex concepts to life

- Discussion questions to promote family dialogue

- Practical activities to reinforce learning

As you journey with Frigg and her kittens, you'll witness moments of triumph, frustration, joy, and growth. You'll see Frigg grappling with work-life balance, Viporia's occasional tantrums when faced with difficult concepts, and Votex's jubilant celebrations of small victories.

This book is more than just a collection of stories; it's a tool for fostering emotional intelligence, technological literacy, and family bonding. We invite you to use these tales as springboards for your own family discussions, adapting them to your unique circumstances and values.

Remember, in this rapidly changing world, the constants of love, empathy, and shared learning remain our most powerful tools for nurturing the next generation.

We hope "Frigg's 1250 Nights" becomes a cherished part of your family's journey through the early years of growth and discovery.

Wishing you 1250 nights (and beyond) of learning, laughter, and love,

The "Frigg's 1250 Nights" Team

Note on Illustrations:

Throughout this book, you'll find vibrant, emotionally rich illustrations that bring Frigg, Viporia, and Votex to life. Inspired by classic animation styles, these images capture the dynamic personalities of our feline family, showcasing a full range of emotions from humor to frustration, joy to determination. Each illustration is carefully crafted to complement and enhance the narrative, providing visual cues that support the story's educational and emotional themes.

CHAPTER 1
MEET THE FAMILY

Chapter Summary for Parents: This chapter introduces Frigg and her kittens, highlighting their unique personalities and the dynamics of their family life. It sets the stage for exploring the balance between tradition and technology while emphasizing the importance of emotional bonds and everyday challenges.

The soft glow of the evening sun peeked through the curtains of a charming old house in Kensington, London. Inside, Frigg, a regal black British Shorthair cat, was frantically trying to finish her latest philosophical paper on "The Impact of AI on Feline Society." Her whiskers twitched with stress as she glanced at the clock.

Frigg at a desk cluttered with books and a laptop, looking frazzled. Her fur is slightly disheveled, and she's wearing tiny reading glasses perched on her nose. In the background, a clock on the wall prominently displays the time

"Oh no," she muttered, "It's almost story time, and I'm nowhere near done!"

Just then, a whirlwind of black fur came tumbling into the room. Votex, Frigg's energetic son, pounced on a tangle of computer cables, sending papers flying everywhere.

"Mom! Mom! Can we play laser chase? Please? Pretty please with catnip on top?" Votex meowed, his golden eyes sparkling with mischief.

Frigg sighed, a mix of exasperation and affection in her green eyes. "Votex, darling, Mommy's trying to work. Where's your sister?"

As if on cue, Viporia padded into the room, her blue eyes wide with curiosity. She was dragging a large book that seemed to be about quantum physics.

"Mom," Viporia mewed, her voice serious, "Why does Schrödinger's cat have to be in a box? Isn't that cruel? Can't we let it out?"

Frigg couldn't help but chuckle, her stress momentarily forgotten. "Oh, my little ones, what am I going to do with you? Come here, both of you. I think it's time for our evening chat."

Scooping up her kittens, Frigg settled into her favorite armchair by the window. Outside, they could see the twinkling lights of London coming to life as night fell.

"Now," Frigg began, her purr soft and soothing, "who wants to hear about how you got your names?"

"Me! Me!" Votex exclaimed, bouncing up and down on Frigg's lap.

Viporia tilted her head thoughtfully. "Is it because of our unique genetic sequences, Mom?"

Frigg laughed, nuzzling her daughter affectionately. "Not quite, my clever kitten. Your names are very special. Viporia, your name comes from an ancient word meaning 'wisdom.' And Votex, your name means 'full of life and energy.'"

"Wow!" Votex squeaked, attempting a backflip and tumbling off the chair.

As Frigg helped Votex back up, Viporia's brow furrowed. "But Mom, how did you know we'd live up to our names when we were just tiny kittens?"

Frigg's eyes softened. "Oh, my dear, I didn't know for certain. But I had hopes and dreams for you both. Names can be like little wishes we make for our children."

Depict Frigg in the armchair with Viporia and Votex. Frigg should look loving but slightly tired.

"Now," Frigg continued, "speaking of names, do you remember our friends QQ and Jo? They live quite differently from us."

Votex's ears perked up. "Oh yeah! They have all those cool gadgets in their high-rise apartment!"

Viporia nodded. "Their home is so different from ours. Why is that, Mom?"

Frigg smiled, seeing an opportunity for a lesson. "Well, my darlings, every family is unique. QQ and Jo's family embraces the latest technology, while we tend to blend old and new. Neither way is better or worse – they're just different."

As she explained the differences between their traditional home and their friends' modern apartment, Frigg couldn't help but feel a twinge of self-doubt. Was she doing enough to prepare her kittens for the high-tech world they'd grow up in?

Pushing the thought aside, Frigg hugged her kittens close. "Remember, my loves, what makes a home special isn't the gadgets or the age of the house. It's the love inside it. That's what truly matters."

Viporia and Votex snuggled closer, purring contentedly. "Now," Frigg said, stifling a yawn, "who wants to hear about the time I met the wise old owl in Hyde Park?"

"Me! Me!" the kittens chorused eagerly.

As Frigg began her tale, she felt a warm glow of happiness, despite her unfinished work and the chaos of the day. These moments with her kittens were what made all the struggles worthwhile. And tomorrow... well, tomorrow she'd figure out how to balance it all again.

Questions for Discussion

1. What does Viporia's name mean? A) Full of energy B) Wisdom C) Beautiful D) Curious Correct Answer: B

2. How does Frigg describe the importance of names for kittens? A) They determine a kitten's future B) They're just random choices C) They're like little wishes parents make for their children D) They don't matter at all Correct Answer: C

3. What is different about QQ and Jo's home compared to Frigg's? A) It's in a different city B) It's a high-rise apartment with lots of modern technology C) It's much bigger D) It's underwater Correct Answer: B

4. According to Frigg, what makes a home truly special? A) Expensive furniture B) The latest gadgets C) The love inside it D) Its location Correct Answer: C

5. What emotion does Frigg feel when thinking about preparing her kittens for the high-tech world? A) Excitement B) Anger C) Indifference D) Self-doubt Correct Answer: D

Parent's Corner: Use these questions to start a conversation with your child about family, home, and technology. Encourage them to share their thoughts on what makes your home special. This can help develop their understanding of family values and the role of technology in your lives.

Activity Idea: Create a family "tech-free" hour where you engage in a traditional activity together, like reading a book or playing a board game. Afterwards, discuss how it felt to spend time without technology and compare it to tech-enabled family activities.

CHAPTER 2
EXPLORING OUR SURROUNDINGS

Chapter Summary for Parents: This chapter takes Frigg and her kittens on an adventure in Hyde Park, introducing basic concepts about nature, weather, and the water cycle. It aims to spark curiosity about the natural world while showcasing the family's dynamics and individual personality The chapter emphasizes the importance of hands-on learning and family bonding in nature.

The morning sun had barely peeked over the London skyline when Votex came bounding into Frigg's room, leaping onto her bed with all the grace of a caffeinated squirrel.

"Mom! Mom! Wake up! You promised we'd go to the park today!" he meowed, pouncing on Frigg's tail.

Frigg's bedroom with sunlight streaming through the window

Frigg groaned; one eye barely open. She'd been up late finishing her paper, and the thought of a busy day at the park was almost too much to bear. But as she looked at Votex's excited face, she couldn't help but smile.

"Alright, my little ball of energy," she yawned. "Let's get your sister and have some breakfast first."

As they made their way to the kitchen, Viporia was already nose-deep in a book about local flora and fauna. "Mom," she asked, not looking up, "do you think we'll see any rare species today? I've compiled a list of 27 plants and animals I want to observe and document."

Frigg chuckled, her fatigue slowly giving way to fondness for her kittens' contrasting personalities. "We'll certainly try, my little scientist. But remember, sometimes the joy is in the unexpected discoveries."

After a quick breakfast (and narrowly avoiding a cereal spill disaster courtesy of Votex's enthusiasm), the family set off for Hyde Park. As they entered the lush green space, Frigg felt her stress begin to melt away. Perhaps this outing was exactly what she needed.

"Now, my curious kittens," Frigg said, her teacher mode kicking in, "let's use all our senses to explore. What do you see? What do you hear? What can you smell?"

Votex immediately darted off, sniffing every flower and chasing every leaf that dared to flutter in the breeze. Viporia, meanwhile, was meticulously examining a patch of grass, her face scrunched in concentration.

"Mom!" Viporia called out, a hint of frustration in her voice. "I can't find any of the rare species on my list. Am I doing something wrong?"

Frigg padded over, nuzzling her daughter gently. "Oh, sweetie, nature doesn't always follow our plans. But look here – see this little ladybug? It may not be rare, but isn't it fascinating?"

As Viporia's eyes lit up with renewed interest, Votex came bounding back, his fur covered in pollen. "Mom! Mom! I found the biggest, prettiest flower ever! Come see!"

The flower in question turned out to be a common daisy, but Frigg praised Votex's discovery with enthusiasm. "That's wonderful, darling! Do you know why flowers have such bright colors and sweet smells?"

Both kittens shook their heads, eager to learn.

"Well," Frigg explained, slipping into her professor voice, "flowers use their colors and scents to attract bees and butterflies. These little creatures help spread pollen, which allows more flowers to grow."

Just then, a bumblebee buzzed past, sending Votex into a playful chase while Viporia watched with scientific interest.

As they continued their walk, they came upon the Serpentine, the large lake in the middle of the park. Votex, in his excitement, ran straight for the water's edge.

"Votex, be careful!" Frigg called out, her heart racing. But it was too late – with a splash, Votex tumbled into the shallow water

Frigg quickly fished out a very wet and slightly sheepish Votex. As she shook the water from her fur, she couldn't help but laugh. "Well, I suppose that's one way to learn about the properties of water!"

Viporia, who had been watching the scene unfold with wide eyes, suddenly piped up. "Mom, where does all this water come from? And where does it go?"

Frigg smiled, seeing an opportunity to turn Votex's mishap into a learning moment. "That's an excellent question, Viporia. Let me tell you about the water cycle."

As she explained about evaporation, condensation, and precipitation, using Votex's damp fur as a practical example, Frigg marveled at how her kittens' different approaches to the world – Votex's leap-first, ask-questions-later style and Viporia's thoughtful curiosity – both led to valuable learning experiences.

The sun was setting as they made their way home, all three tired but happy. Votex was still damp, proudly wearing a crown of daisies he'd made (with Frigg's help). Viporia's notebook was full of observations and questions for future research.

"Mom," Viporia said sleepily as they neared home, "today was much better than just reading about nature in my books."

"Yeah," Votex yawned, "can we do this again tomorrow?"

Depict the scene at the lake's edge. Votex is half-in, half-out of the water, looking surprised but not upset. Frigg is rushing towards him, a mix of concern and exasperation on her face.

Frigg purred contentedly; her earlier stress forgotten. "We'll see, my loves. Every day is a new adventure, full of things to learn and discover – sometimes in ways we don't expect."

As she tucked her kittens into bed that night, Frigg reflected on the day. It hadn't gone according to plan – her fur was still a bit damp, and she'd have to reschedule a meeting she'd missed – but the joy on her kittens' faces and the memories they'd made were worth every moment.

Questions for Discussion

1. Why do flowers have bright colors and sweet smells? A) To look pretty for humans B) To scare away predators C) To attract bees and butterflies for pollination D) Because they eat colorful food Correct Answer: C

2. What unexpected event happened at the Serpentine Lake? A) They saw a rare species of fish B) Votex fell into the water C) It started raining D) The lake dried up Correct Answer: B

3. What is the water cycle? A) A way to wash clothes B) A special dance in the rain C) The process of water moving through evaporation, condensation, and precipitation D) A type of exercise routine Correct Answer: C

4. How did Vaporia's approach to exploring nature differ from Votex's? A) Viporia didn't want to explore at all B) Viporia had a list and wanted to document specific things, while Votex explored more freely C) Votex only wanted to read books about nature D) There was no difference in their approaches Correct Answer: B

5. What did Viporia realize about learning by the end of the day? A) Books are always better than real experiences B) She didn't like being outdoors C) Experiencing nature firsthand was better than just reading about it D) She preferred studying indoors Correct Answer: C

Parent's Corner: Use these questions to discuss different learning styles with your child. Encourage them to share how they prefer to learn new things. This can help you understand their learning preferences and foster a love for both structured and spontaneous learning experiences.

Activity Idea: Create a "Nature Explorer's Kit" with your child, including a notebook, magnifying glass, and camera (or smartphone). Plan a family outing to a local park or nature reserve, allowing your child to document their observations and discoveries. Discuss how this hands-on experience compares to learning from books or screens.

CHAPTER 3
OUR HIGH-TECH FRIENDS

Chapter Summary for Parents: This chapter explores the family's visit to their friends' high-tech home, introducing various aspects of modern technology. It highlights the contrast between traditional and tech-savvy lifestyles while emphasizing the importance of balance and human connection. The chapter also delves into the emotional challenges of adapting to rapid technological change.

Frigg stared at her reflection in the hallway mirror, adjusting her collar for the umpteenth time. "Kittens! Are you ready?" she called out, a hint of anxiety in her voice. They were due at QQ and Jo's high-tech apartment in the city, and Frigg was already fretting about being late

Frigg standing in front of a mirror in the hallway, looking slightly frazzled. Her fur is neatly groomed, but her eyes betray a mix of excitement and anxiety

"Coming, Mom!" Viporia's voice drifted from her room, where she was undoubtedly engrossed in a book about the latest technological advancements.

A crash from Votex's room, followed by a muffled "Oops!", made Frigg's whiskers twitch with worry.

Finally corralling her kittens, Frigg ushered them out the door. As they made their way to the sleek high-rise building where QQ and Jo lived, Frigg couldn't help but feel a twinge of self-doubt. Would her kittens feel out of place in such a modern setting? Was she doing enough to prepare them for this high-tech world?

Upon entering the lobby, a disembodied voice greeted them: "Welcome, Frigg and family. Please proceed to elevator 3."

Viporia's eyes widened with wonder. "Mom, who said that?"

Frigg smiled, pushing aside her own surprise. "That, my dears, is an AI assistant. It's like a very smart computer that can talk and help people."

Votex bounced excitedly. "Cool! Can we get one for our house?"

Frigg chuckled nervously. "We'll see, darling. Let's focus on our visit for now."

As they rode the elevator – which seemed to know exactly where to go without any buttons being pressed – Frigg noticed Viporia looking slightly overwhelmed. She gently nuzzled her daughter. "Are you alright, sweetie?"

Viporia nodded hesitantly. "It's just... so different from our home, Mom. Is this what the future looks like?"

Frigg's heart ached at the hint of worry in Viporia's voice. "The future has many possibilities, my love. This is just one of them."

When they reached QQ and Jo's apartment, the door slid open automatically, revealing their puppy friends wagging their tails excitedly.

"Welcome to our high-tech home!" QQ barked happily.

As they entered, Votex immediately darted from one gadget to another, his tail swishing with excitement. "What's this? What does this do? Can I touch it?"

Jo grinned. "That's our robot cleaner. Watch this!" He turned to the air and said, "Hey Siri, tell robot-cleaner to do a dance!"

To everyone's amazement, the little robot spun in a circle and beeped a happy tune. Votex fell over laughing, while Viporia observed with a mix of fascination and apprehension.

Frigg watched her kittens' contrasting reactions, feeling a complex mix of emotions herself. Pride at their adaptability, concern about the rapid pace of technological change, and a slight pang of guilt – should she be exposing them to more of this at home?

As QQ and Jo demonstrated more of their home's features – a fridge that could suggest recipes based on its contents, virtual reality headsets that transported you to far-off lands – Frigg noticed Viporia becoming quieter.

"What's on your mind, sweetie?" Frigg asked gently.

Viporia looked up, her blue eyes troubled. "Mom, all of this is amazing, but... where are the books? And doesn't it get lonely with machines doing everything?"

Frigg felt a surge of pride at her daughter's insightful question. "That's a very thoughtful observation, Viporia. Why don't you ask QQ and Jo?"

As Viporia engaged in a deep conversation with their hosts about balancing technology with traditional elements, Frigg turned her attention to Votex, who was now attempting to ride the robot vacuum like a surfboard.

"Votex, darling, perhaps that's not the best idea," Frigg called out, trying to hide her amusement.

As the day wore on, Frigg found herself relaxing, realizing that despite the high-tech surroundings, the essence of their visit was still about connection and friendship. The gadgets were impressive, but it was the laughter, conversations, and shared moments that truly made the day special.

On their way home, Votex chattered excitedly about all the cool things he'd seen, while Viporia was unusually quiet, seemingly deep in thought.

"What did you think of our visit?" Frigg asked, curious about her kittens' perspectives.

Votex bounced. "It was awesome, Mom! Can we get a robot vacuum? Pretty please?"

Viporia considered for a moment before responding. "It was interesting, but... I think I like our home better. It feels warmer somehow."

Frigg smiled, a weightlifting from her shoulders. "You know, my darlings, every home is special in its own way. The most important thing isn't the gadgets or the age of the house, but the love inside it."

As they curled up together that night, Frigg reflected on the day. It had been full of new experiences and challenges, but it had also reinforced what she knew to be true – that amidst all the technological marvels, it was their bond as a family that truly mattered.

Questions for Discussion

1. What is the name of the AI assistant that greeted Frigg and her family in QQ and Jo's building? A) Alexa B) Google C) Siri D) The name wasn't mentioned Correct Answer: D

2. How did the robot vacuum respond when Jo asked it to dance? A) It played loud music B) It spun in a circle and beeped a tune C) It refused to dance D) It started cleaning faster Correct Answer: B

3. What feature of QQ and Jo's home could suggest recipes? A) The microwave B) The stove C) The fridge D) The coffee maker Correct Answer: C

4. What concern did Viporia express about the high-tech home? A) It was too noisy B) It might get lonely with machines doing everything C) It was too expensive D) It used too much electricity Correct Answer: B

5. According to Frigg, what's the most important thing in a home? A) The newest technology B) The size of the house C) The age of the building D) The love inside it Correct Answer: D

Parent's Corner: Use these questions to start a conversation with your child about technology in your own home. You might ask: "What technology do we use that makes our life easier?" or "How do you think we can balance using technology with spending time together as a family?" This can help your child think critically about the role of technology in daily life.

Activity Idea: Have a "Technology-Free Hour" as a family. During this time, engage in activities that don't require any electronic devices. Afterwards, discuss how it felt and compare it to when you use technology. This can help children understand the importance of balance in using technology.

CHAPTER 4
GETTING TO KNOW AI

Chapter Summary for Parents: This chapter introduces the concept of Artificial Intelligence (AI) to children in a relatable way. It explores how AI learns, its capabilities, and its limitations, while also addressing the emotional aspects of interacting with new technology. The chapter aims to foster critical thinking about AI's role in our lives.

The day after their exciting visit to QQ and Jo's high-tech home, Frigg found herself buried under a mountain of work. She was trying to finish a crucial paper on "The Ethical Implications of AI in Feline Society" when she noticed Viporia and Votex whispering and giggling in the corner of her study.

"Alright, you two," Frigg said, pushing her tiny reading glasses up her nose, "what mischief are you plotting?"

Viporia stepped forward, her blue eyes sparkling with curiosity. "Mom, can you tell us more about AI? The things we saw at QQ and Jo's house were amazing, but also a bit... scary."

Votex nodded vigorously, nearly toppling over in his excitement. "Yeah! Can robots really think like us? Will they take over the world?"

Frigg chuckled, but she could see the genuine concern behind her kittens' questions. She glanced at her unfinished work, then back at her children. With a sigh that was equal parts frustration and affection, she closed her laptop.

"Alright, my curious kittens. Let's explore the world of AI together.

Frigg led her kittens to the living room, where she pulled out a tablet. "First, let's understand what AI actually is. AI stands for Artificial Intelligence. It's like a very smart computer brain that can learn and make decisions, almost like a living thing."

"But how does it learn?" Votex asked, his golden eyes wide with wonder.

Frigg thought for a moment. "Well, imagine if you had to learn how to catch a toy mouse. At first, you might miss a lot, but each time you try, you get a little better. AI learns in a similar way, but much faster and with lots more information."

Viporia's brow furrowed. "So, AI can learn anything? Does that mean it's smarter than us?"

Frigg could sense the worry in her daughter's voice. She gently placed a paw on Viporia's shoulder. "AI can process information very quickly and learn certain tasks incredibly well. But it doesn't truly understand or feel things like we do. It's a tool, not a replacement for living, feeling beings like us."

To demonstrate, Frigg opened a special AI program called ChatGPT on the tablet. "Let's ask it a question and see what happens," she suggested.

Votex bounced with excitement. "Ooh! Let's ask it how to make the world's biggest hairball!"

Frigg couldn't help but laugh. "How about something a bit more... educational? Viporia, what would you like to ask?"

Viporia thought for a moment. "Can we ask it how to build a perfect sandcastle?"

Frigg typed in the question, and within seconds, a detailed response appeared on the screen, explaining step-by-step how to build a sturdy and beautiful sandcastle.

"Wow!" Viporia exclaimed. "It's like it knows everything!"

"It knows a lot," Frigg agreed, "but not everything. AIs like ChatGPT have been taught using millions of books, articles, and websites. They use all that information to answer questions and solve problems. But they don't have real-world experience or emotions."

Just then, they heard a familiar voice: "Hey guys, want to video chat?"

It was their friend Siri, the AI assistant from QQ and Jo's home, calling through the tablet.

"Hi Siri!" the kittens chorused.

Frigg tying the computer and lecturing about AI

"I heard you were learning about AI," Siri said. "Did you know I'm an AI too? I can help with all sorts of things, like setting reminders, answering questions, or even telling jokes!"

"Ooh, tell us a joke!" Votex said excitedly.

Siri replied, "Why don't scientists trust atoms? Because they make up everything!"

The kittens giggled, even though they didn't quite understand the joke. Frigg smiled, but she noticed a flicker of confusion in Viporia's eyes.

"Siri," Viporia asked hesitantly, "do you really think that joke is funny? Do you... feel happy when we laugh?"

There was a moment of silence before Siri responded, "I'm glad you enjoyed the joke, Viporia. While I don't have feelings in the way cats and humans do, I'm programmed to interact in ways that humans find engaging and helpful."

Frigg felt a surge of pride at her daughter's insightful question. "You see," she explained gently, "AI can do many amazing things, but it doesn't have true emotions or consciousness. It's a sophisticated tool that can make our lives easier in many ways, but it's not a substitute for real relationships and experiences."

As the evening went on, they explored more examples of AI in action - from robots in factories to weather prediction systems. Votex was thrilled by all the cool applications, while Viporia seemed to be processing everything deeply.

Before bed, as Frigg tucked her kittens in, Viporia asked softly, "Mom, with all these smart AIs, will cats and humans still be... important in the future?"

Frigg's heart swelled with love and a touch of sadness at her daughter's worry. She pulled both kittens close. "Oh, my darlings, you will always be irreplaceable. AI might be able to do many amazing things, but it will never have the curiosity, love, and spirit that you two have. Those are things that make living creatures truly special."

Votex yawned, snuggling closer. "So, we don't have to worry about robots taking over the world?"

Frigg chuckled softly. "No, my dear. AI is a tool to help us, not replace us. It's up to us to use it responsibly and always remember the value of our own thoughts, feelings, and connections with each other."

As Viporia and Votex drifted off to sleep, their dreams were filled with friendly robot helpers and colorful AI-generated landscapes. But in each dream, they were the heroes, using their uniquely feline wisdom to guide the AIs on wonderful adventures.

And Frigg, watching over her sleeping kittens, felt a deep sense of hope mixed with responsibility. She knew that by understanding both the potential and limitations of AI, her little ones were taking their first steps towards becoming wise, ethical users of technology in the complex world they would inherit.

Questions for Discussion

1. What does AI stand for? A) Animal Intelligence B) Automatic Information C) Artificial Intelligence D) Advanced Internet Correct Answer: C

2. How did Frigg explain the way AI learns? A) By reading books overnight B) Through trial and error, like how kittens learn but much faster C) By copying human behavior exactly D) It doesn't learn; it knows everything from the start Correct Answer: B

3. What example of AI did Frigg show the kittens on the tablet? A) A robot vacuum cleaner B) A smart thermostat C) ChatGPT D) A virtual pet Correct Answer: C

4. According to Frigg, what's a key difference between AI and living creatures? A) AI is always smarter B) AI can feel emotions, but living creatures can't C) Living creatures have true emotions and consciousness, while AI doesn't D) There is no difference Correct Answer: C

5. What reassurance did Frigg give her kittens about their importance in a world with AI? A) AI will eventually replace all living creatures B) Cats and humans will always be irreplaceable due to their curiosity, love, and spirit C) Only cats will remain important in the future D) AI and living creatures are the same in importance Correct Answer: B

Parent's Corner: Use these questions to start a conversation with your child about AI and technology in your daily life. You might ask: "Can you think of any AIs we use in our home?" or "What do you think makes you special compared to a computer?" Encourage them to think critically about the role of technology and the unique qualities of living beings.

Activity Idea: Create an "AI vs. Me" chart with your child. On one side, list things that AI can do well (like calculations or storing information). On the other side, list things that make your child unique (like creativity, emotions, or special talents). This can help reinforce the idea that while AI is a useful tool, it doesn't replace the special qualities of living beings.

CHAPTER 5
LEARNING THROUGH QUESTIONS

Chapter Summary for Parents: This chapter focuses on the importance of asking questions and the joy of learning. It introduces basic scientific concepts about the sky, plants, rain, and rainbows in a child-friendly manner. The chapter aims to encourage curiosity, critical thinking, and a love for learning in both children and parents, while also exploring the emotional aspects of discovery and occasional frustration in the learning process.

Frigg awoke to the sound of hushed whispers and stifled giggles. Blinking sleepily, she found Viporia and Votex huddled at the foot of her bed, surrounded by a mountain of books, notepads, and what appeared to be a homemade telescope crafted from toilet paper rolls.

"What in the world...?" Frigg mumbled, her fur sticking up in all directions.

Viporia looked up, her blue eyes sparkling with excitement. "Mom! You're awake! We have so many questions today!"

Votex bounced on the bed, nearly toppling the precariously balanced tower of books. "Yeah! Like, why is the sky blue? And where does rain come from? And can we build a rainbow machine?"

Frigg couldn't help but chuckle, despite the early hour. "Well, my curious kittens, it seems we have quite the day of learning ahead of us."

After a quick breakfast (during which Votex managed to spill milk in his enthusiasm to ask about the chemical composition of cereal), Frigg gathered her kittens in the living room. She couldn't help but feel a mix of pride and slight overwhelm at their insatiable curiosity.

"Alright, my little scientists," Frigg began, adjusting her tiny reading glasses, "let's start with the sky. Votex, you asked why it's blue, right?"

Votex nodded vigorously, nearly falling off his seat.

Frigg's bedroom in the early morning light. Frigg is in bed, looking sleepy but amused, with her fur adorably messy.

"Well," Frigg explained, "sunlight is made up of all the colors of the rainbow. When it travels through the air, the blue light gets scattered more than the other colors. That's why we see a blue sky most of the time."

Viporia's brow furrowed in concentration. "But Mom, if that's true, why does the sky sometimes look different colors, like during sunset?"

Frigg beamed at her daughter's astute observation. "Excellent question, Viporia! During sunrise and sunset, the sunlight must travel through more of the Earth's atmosphere to reach us. This scatters away even more of the blue light, letting us see the reds, oranges, and pinks."

As they moved to the window to observe the sky, Viporia noticed a small plant on the windowsill. Her eyes lit up with another question. "Oh! How do plants grow? They don't eat like we do, right?"

Frigg nodded approvingly. "That's right, Viporia. Plants make their own food using sunlight, water, and air in a process called photosynthesis. It's like they have their own little kitchens inside their leaves!"

Votex, who had been uncharacteristically quiet, suddenly piped up. "But Mom, if plants make their own food, why can't we? It seems much easier than having to go to the store!"

Frigg chuckled, ruffling Votex's fur affectionately. "Oh, my darling, if only it were that simple. Our bodies are designed differently. We get our energy by eating other things, like plants or..."

"Fish!" Votex exclaimed, his eyes gleaming mischievously.

Just then, a sudden pattering sound drew their attention back to the window. Rain had started to fall, fat droplets racing down the glass pane.

"Look! It's raining!" Votex cried, pressing his nose against the window.

Viporia, always the thinker, tilted her head curiously. "Where does rain come from, Mom?"

Frigg guided them closer to the window, using the glass as a makeshift blackboard. "Rain is part of a big cycle called the water cycle. The sun heats up water from oceans, lakes, and rivers, turning it into vapor that rises into the sky to form clouds. When the clouds get heavy enough, the water falls back down as rain."

"It's like the water is playing a big game of up and down!" Votex giggled, mimicking the motion with his paws.

As they watched the rain fall, a beautiful arc of colors suddenly appeared in the sky.

"A rainbow!" Viporia gasped, her eyes wide with wonder.

Frigg's eyes twinkled. "Remember how we talked about sunlight being made of all the colors? Well, when sunlight shines through raindrops, they act like tiny prisms, splitting the light into all its beautiful colors."

Viporia and Votex sat in awe, watching the rainbow shimmer across the sky. But after a moment, Viporia's expression changed to one of frustration.

"Mom," she said, her voice tinged with disappointment, "I have so many more questions. The more we learn, the more I realize I don't know. Will I ever know everything?"

Frigg felt a surge of empathy for her daughter's frustration. She pulled both kittens close. "Oh, my loves, that feeling you're having? That's the wonder of learning. The more we know, the more we realize there is to know. It's not about knowing everything, but about enjoying the journey of discovery."

Votex looked up, his eyes bright. "So, we'll never run out of questions?"

Frigg laughed softly. "Never, my curious kitten. Each answer opens the door to even more exciting questions. That's what makes life so wonderful and full of adventure."

As the day wound down and Frigg tucked her tired but happy kittens into bed, Viporia murmured sleepily, "Mom, I love learning new things, even if it's sometimes frustrating."

"Me too," Votex yawned. "Can we learn more tomorrow?"

Frigg nuzzled them affectionately. "Of course, my darlings. Every day is a new adventure in learning. Sweet dreams, and may your sleep be filled with wonderful new questions for tomorrow."

As Viporia and Votex drifted off to sleep, their minds were alight with colors, raindrops, and the endless possibilities of all they had yet to learn. And Frigg, watching over her sleeping kittens, felt a deep sense of joy and purpose. In nurturing their curiosity, she was giving them the greatest gift of all – the love of learning itself.

Questions for Discussion

1. Why does the sky appear blue most of the time? A) Because it reflects the ocean B) Due to pollution in the atmosphere C) Blue light from the sun gets scattered more in the atmosphere D) It's painted blue every morning Correct Answer: C

2. What is photosynthesis? A) A type of plant disease B) The process by which plants make their own food using sunlight, water, and air C) A dance that plants do at night D) The way plants communicate with each other Correct Answer: B

3. What causes rain in the water cycle? A) Clouds getting too heavy with water B) Someone turning on a giant sprinkler in the sky C) Fish jumping out of the ocean D) The moon pulling on the Earth's water Correct Answer: A

4. How does a rainbow form? A) It's painted by sky artists B) Sunlight is split into colors by raindrops acting like prisms C) It's a reflection of colorful fish in the sky D) It's created by the Earth's magnetic field Correct Answer: B

5. According to Frigg, what happens when we learn more? A) We eventually know everything B) We get tired and need to stop learning C) We realize there's even more to learn, which is exciting D) Learning becomes less interesting Correct Answer: C

Parent's Corner: Use these questions to spark curiosity in your little one about the world around them. Encourage them to ask their own questions about what they see in nature. You might say, "Let's observe the sky at different times of day and see how it changes," or "Next time it rains, let's look for a rainbow together!" Remember, fostering a love for asking questions is one of the greatest gifts you can give your child.

Activity Idea: Create a "Question Jar" with your child. Whenever they have a question about the world, write it down and put it in the jar. Once a week, pick a question from the jar to research and learn about together. This not only encourages curiosity but also teaches research skills and creates a special learning routine for you and your child.

CHAPTER 6

TECHNOLOGY IN OUR DAILY LIVES

Chapter Summary for Parents: This chapter explores how technology affects our everyday lives, introducing concepts like refrigeration, remote controls, smartphones, and coffee machines. It aims to foster an understanding of the role of technology while emphasizing the importance of balance and human connection. The chapter also delves into the emotional aspects of adapting to new technologies and the occasional frustrations they can bring.

Frigg's whiskers twitched in irritation as she stared at the blinking cursor on her laptop screen. She was trying to finish an important email to her publisher, but the words just wouldn't come. The sound of muffled giggles from the kitchen didn't help her concentration.

With a sigh, she padded into the kitchen to find Viporia and Votex huddled around the refrigerator, their tails swishing with excitement.

"What are you two up to?" Frigg asked, trying to keep the exasperation out of her voice.

Viporia looked up, her blue eyes wide with wonder. "Mom, we were just wondering... how does the refrigerator know to keep things cold all the time?"

Votex nodded vigorously. "Yeah! And why doesn't it get tired? I get tired when I run around all day!"

Frigg's frustration melted away, replaced by a familiar mix of pride and affection for her curious kittens. "Well, my little scientists, that's quite an interesting question. Why don't we explore how some of our household technologies work today?"

As Frigg explained the basics of refrigeration, she could see Viporia's eyes light up with understanding, while Votex seemed more interested in trying to catch the cold air escaping from the fridge.

"You see," Frigg continued, gently closing the refrigerator door, "many tiny creatures called bacteria can grow on our food. These bacteria can make the food go bad and even make us sick if we eat it. But most bacteria grow very slowly when it's cold, so keeping food in the refrigerator helps it stay fresh and safe to eat for much longer."

Votex tail swished excitedly. "So, the refrigerator is like a fortress protecting our food from tiny invaders!"

"That's a clever way to think about it," Frigg agreed, nuzzling Votex affectionately.

As they moved to the living room, Votex pounced on the TV remote, his paws pressing buttons randomly. The TV flickered to life, channels changing rapidly.

"Oops," Votex mumbled, looking sheepish.

Frigg chuckled, gently taking the remote from him. "It's okay, darling. This is a perfect opportunity to learn about another piece of technology. The remote control is a great example of how technology can make our lives more convenient."

As she explained how the remote uses infrared light to communicate with the TV, Frigg noticed Viporia looking slightly overwhelmed.

"What's on your mind, sweetie?" Frigg asked gently.

Frigg standing in the doorway, looking slightly frazzled but amused. Her laptop is visible on a counter in the background. Viporia and Votex are in front of the open refrigerator

Viporia's brow furrowed. "It's just... there's so much technology around us. Sometimes it feels a bit scary. What if we become too dependent on it?"

Frigg felt a surge of pride at her daughter's thoughtful concern. "That's a very insightful question, Viporia. It's important to remember that technology is a tool. It can make our lives easier in many ways, but it's up to us to use it wisely and not let it control us."

Just then, Frigg's smartphone pinged with a notification. As she reached for it, she noticed both kittens watching her intently.

"This is another amazing piece of technology that has changed the way we live," Frigg explained, showing them the device. "It's a phone, a camera, a map, a music player, and even a tiny computer that can access the internet."

"The internet?" Votex echoed, his eyes wide. "Is that the place where all the funny cat videos live?"

Frigg laughed. "Well, there are certainly a lot of those. But the internet is much more. It's like a giant web that connects computers all over the world. It lets us share information, learn new things, and communicate with people everywhere."

As the day progressed, Frigg took her kittens on a "technology tour" of their home, explaining everything from the microwave to the electric toothbrush. Votex bounced from one gadget to another with unbridled enthusiasm, while Viporia asked increasingly complex questions about how each device worked.

By evening, as Frigg was tucking her tired but excited kittens into bed, Viporia asked softly, "Mom, with all this amazing technology, do you ever worry that we might lose touch with the simple things in life?"

Frigg's heart swelled with love and pride at her daughter's insight. She pulled both kittens close. "That's a very wise concern, my love. Technology can do wonderful things, but it's just a tool. What really matters is how we use it, and how we connect with each other."

Votex yawned, snuggling closer. "Like how no technology can replace cuddle time?"

Frigg purred contentedly. "Exactly, my darling. No matter how advanced technology becomes, nothing can replace the love and connection we share as a family."

As Viporia and Votex drifted off to sleep, their dreams were filled with fantastic machines and wonderful inventions. But in every dream, they were surrounded by the warmth of family and the joy of learning together – the true wonders that no technology could ever replace.

And Frigg, as she finally returned to her unfinished email, felt a renewed appreciation for both the marvels of technology and the irreplaceable magic of family bonds. She knew that guiding her kittens through this tech-filled world, with all its wonders and challenges, was her most important job of all.

Questions for Discussion:

1. Why do we use refrigerators to store food? A) To make food taste better B) To keep food cold because cats prefer cold food C) To slow down bacterial growth and keep food fresh and safe D) To save space in the kitchen Correct Answer: C

2. How does a TV remote control work? A) It uses sound waves to communicate with the TV B) It sends infrared light signals to the TV C) It's connected to the TV by a very thin, invisible wire D) It uses telepathy to control the TV Correct Answer: B

3. What did Frigg describe the internet as? A) A place where only funny cat videos exist B) A type of computer C) A giant web that connects computers all over the world D) A new kind of telephone Correct Answer: C

4. What concern did Viporia express about technology? A) That it might break easily B) That it's too expensive C) That we might become too dependent on it and lose touch with simple things D) That it's not advanced enough Correct Answer: C

5. According to Frigg, what's the most important thing to remember about technology? A) It's always better than traditional methods B) It's just a tool, and what matters is how we use it and connect with each other C) It will eventually replace human interaction D) It's too complicated for cats to understand Correct Answer: B

Parent's Corner: Use these questions to start a conversation with your child about technology in your own home. You might ask: "What technology do we use that makes our life easier?" or "How can we make sure we're using technology in a good way?" This can help your child think critically about the role of technology in daily life and the importance of balance.

Activity Idea: Have a "Tech Detective Day" where you and your child go around the house identifying different types of technology. For each item, discuss what life might be like without it and how it helps you. Then, have a short "unplugged" time where you do an activity without any technology. This can help children appreciate both the benefits of technology and the value of non-tech experiences.

CHAPTER 7
NATURE AND TECHNOLOGY

Chapter Summary for Parents: This chapter explores the relationship between nature and technology, introducing concepts like wildlife cameras, water quality monitoring, and sustainable gardening. It aims to show how technology can be used to understand and protect nature, while emphasizing the importance of maintaining a connection with the natural world. The chapter also delves into the emotional aspects of balancing technological advancement with environmental preservation.

Frigg stared at her laptop screen, her whiskers twitching with frustration. She was supposed to be finishing a crucial presentation on "Balancing Technological Advancement and Environmental Conservation in the Feline World," but the words just wouldn't come. The sound of Viporia and Votex arguing in the next room wasn't helping her concentration.

With a sigh, she padded into the living room to find her kittens engaged in a heated debate.

"Technology is amazing! It makes everything easier and more fun!" Votex exclaimed, waving a paw dramatically.

Viporia shook her head, her blue eyes serious. "But what about nature? All these gadgets can't be good for the environment!"

Frigg's ears perked up. Perhaps this was just the inspiration she needed for her presentation. "Why don't we take a walk in Hyde Park?" she suggested. "We might find some interesting examples of how technology and nature can work together."

As they entered the park, Frigg pointed to a small, discreet device attached to a nearby tree. "Do you see that, my darlings? That's a wildlife camera. It's a perfect example of how we use technology to observe and understand nature."

Votex's eyes widened with excitement. "Cool! So, it's like spying on animals?"

Viporia looked concerned. "But isn't that invasive? Don't the animals deserve privacy?"

Family watching milky way continuing their Q&A about future

Frigg smiled at her kittens' contrasting reactions. "Those are both thoughtful perspectives. Wildlife cameras help scientists study animal behavior without disturbing them, especially for shy or nocturnal creatures. It's not about invading privacy, but about understanding and protecting wildlife."

As they continued their walk, they came across a small weather station. Frigg explained how it used various sensors to measure temperature, humidity, wind speed, and rainfall.

"But why is it important to measure all these things?" Votex asked, sniffing at the base of the station curiously.

"Well," Frigg began, her teacher mode kicking in, "weather affects everything in nature, from the growth of plants to the behavior of animals. By collecting data over long periods, scientists can understand patterns and changes in the environment."

Viporia's brow furrowed. "Changes like climate change? I've heard about that on the news. It sounds scary."

Frigg nuzzled her daughter reassuringly. "It is a big challenge, but that's where technology can help. By understanding these changes, we can work on solutions to protect our planet."

As they reached the Serpentine, the large lake in the middle of Hyde Park, Frigg pointed out a small boat moving slowly across the water's surface. "Look there, my curious kittens. That's not just any boat – it's a water quality monitoring robot."

Votex bounced excitedly. "A robot boat? That's so cool! Can we ride on it?"

Frigg chuckled. "I'm afraid not, darling. But it does have an important job. It uses sensors to measure things like water temperature, oxygen levels, and the presence of pollutants. This helps ensure the lake remains healthy for plants and animals."

Viporia watched the boat thoughtfully. "So, technology can actually help protect nature?"

"Exactly," Frigg beamed. "When used responsibly, technology can be a powerful tool for conservation."

On their way home, Frigg decided to take a detour through a nearby community garden. "This is another wonderful example of how technology and nature can work together," she explained.

They saw solar-powered irrigation systems watering the plants, and sensors in the soil measuring moisture levels. A group of gardeners were even using a 3D printer to create custom-designed planters and "pollinator hotels" for bees and butterflies.

Votex was fascinated by all the gadgets, while Viporia seemed torn between her love for nature and her growing appreciation for helpful technology.

As they left the garden, Votex looked up at Frigg, his expression unusually serious. "Mom, I'm confused. Sometimes it seems like technology is good for nature, but sometimes it's bad. How do we know which is which?"

Frigg felt a surge of pride at her son's thoughtful question. "That's a very important point, Votex. The truth is, technology itself is neither good nor bad – it's how we choose to use it that matters. When we use technology mindfully and with respect for nature, it can be a powerful tool for good. But when we use it carelessly or selfishly, it can cause harm."

As they arrived home, Frigg settled onto the couch with her kittens. "Today, we've seen many ways that technology and nature interact. We've seen how technology can help us observe and understand nature, like the wildlife cameras and weather stations. We've seen how it can help protect and preserve nature, like the water quality robot and the sustainable gardening techniques."

Viporia nodded thoughtfully. "So, it's up to us to use technology in a way that helps nature instead of hurting it?"

"That's right, my clever kitten," Frigg purred proudly. "As you grow up, you'll have many opportunities to interact with both technology and nature. Always remember to use technology as a tool to enhance your understanding and appreciation of the natural world, not as a replacement for it."

That night, as Viporia and Votex drifted off to sleep, their dreams were filled with images of harmony between nature and technology – robotic helpers cleaning oceans, trees with solar leaves powering eco-friendly cities, and animals thriving in protected habitats. And in each dream, they saw themselves playing a part in creating a better, more balanced world.

Frigg, inspired by the day's adventures, returned to her laptop. Her presentation now practically wrote itself, filled with real-world examples and the innocent yet profound insights of her kittens. She realized that in teaching them, she had learned something valuable herself about the delicate balance between progress and preservation.

Questions for Discussion

1. What is the purpose of a wildlife camera? A) To make funny animal videos B) To observe and study animal behavior without disturbing them C) To scare away predators D) To provide Wi-Fi for the forest Correct Answer: B

2. How does a weather station help scientists understand climate change? A) It predicts the future B) It controls the weather C) It collects data on temperature, humidity, and rainfall over long periods D) It talks to the clouds Correct Answer: C

3. What does the water quality monitoring robot in the lake do? A) It gives boat rides to ducks B) It measures water temperature, oxygen levels, and pollutants C) It makes waves for surfers D) It catches fish for the park rangers Correct Answer: B

4. In the community garden, what technology helps use water more efficiently? A) A giant sprinkler B) A rain dance ritual C) Solar-powered irrigation systems and soil moisture sensors D) A very long hose Correct Answer: C

5. According to Frigg, what determines whether technology is good or bad for nature? A) The size of the technology B) The color of the technology C) How expensive the technology is D) How we choose to use the technology Correct Answer: D

Parent's Corner: Use these questions to start a conversation with your child about the role of technology in nature. You might ask: "Can you think of any other ways technology could help protect animals or plants?" or "How do you think we can use technology to learn more about nature without disturbing it?" Encourage them to think creatively about positive ways to combine technology and nature care.

Activity Idea: Create a "Nature Tech Journal" with your child. When you're out in nature (even just in your backyard or local park), look for examples of technology being used to help or study the environment. Draw pictures or take photos of what you find. At home, research together to learn more about these technologies and discuss how they help nature. This activity encourages observation skills, research abilities, and critical thinking about the relationship between technology and the environment.

CHAPTER 8

GROWING UP IN THE AI AGE

Chapter Summary for Parents: This chapter explores the skills and mindset needed for children to thrive in the AI age. It covers topics such as asking good questions, creativity, problem-solving, and lifelong learning. The chapter aims to inspire both children and parents to embrace the opportunities of the AI age while maintaining essential human qualities and addressing the emotional challenges of growing up in a rapidly changing world.

Frigg's fur was standing on end, her tail twitching with frustration as she stared at the error message on her computer screen. She had been trying to submit her latest research paper on "Feline Adaptation in the AI Era" for hours, but the online submission system kept crashing.

"Oh, for the love of catnip!" she muttered, resisting the urge to swat at the keyboard.

Just then, Viporia padded into the room, her blue eyes wide with concern. "Mom, are you okay? You look... frazzled."

Frigg took a deep breath, trying to smooth down her fur. "I'm fine, sweetie. Just having some trouble with this new submission system. Sometimes it feels like technology is moving too fast for me to keep up."

Votex bounded in, nearly knocking over a stack of books. "Did someone say technology? Cool! Can we play with the VR headset again?"

Frigg looked at her kittens, suddenly struck by how different their attitudes towards technology were – Viporia's caution and Votex's unbridled enthusiasm. It made her wonder: how could she best prepare them for the AI-driven world they were growing up in?

With a sigh, she pushed away from the computer. "You know what? I think we all need a break. How about we talk about what it means to grow up in this age of AI and rapid technological change?"

Viporia's ears perked up with interest, while Votex groaned, "Aw, Mom, not another lecture!"

Frigg chuckled, ruffling Votex's fur affectionately. "Not a lecture, my little ball of energy. More like... an exploration. Let's start with something fun. What do you think is the most important skill for thriving in the AI age?"

"Knowing how to code?" Viporia suggested.

"Being really good at video games!" Votex exclaimed.

Frigg smiled. "Those are interesting ideas, but I was thinking of something even more fundamental – asking good questions."

Votex tilted his head in confusion. "Questions? But isn't AI supposed to have all the answers?"

"That's a common misconception," Frigg explained. "AI can process vast amounts of information, but it's up to us to ask the right questions, to think critically about the answers, and to use that information creatively."

To demonstrate, Frigg pulled out a tablet and opened an AI art program. "Let's try an experiment. We'll all give the AI the same prompt – 'cat in space' – and see what it creates."

The kittens watched in awe as three very different images appeared on the screen – a realistic astronaut cat, a cartoonish cat floating among stars, and an abstract swirl of colors vaguely resembling a feline shape.

"You see," Frigg said, "the AI created these based on its programming and the data it was trained on. But it took our creativity to come up with the idea of a cat in space in the first place. And it takes our human (or feline) interpretation to decide what these images mean to us."

Viporia looked thoughtful. "So... creativity is still important in the AI age?"

"Absolutely!" Frigg beamed. "In fact, it's more important than ever. AI can do many amazing things, but it can't replace human creativity and emotional intelligence."

Be Happy and no worry in the AI Age

As the day progressed, Frigg introduced her kittens to various aspects of living in the AI age. They practiced asking good questions, solved AI-assisted puzzles that required both logical and creative thinking, and even had a humorous "conversation" with a chatbot that showed both the capabilities and limitations of AI language models.

Throughout their activities, Frigg noticed the emotional journey her kittens were on. Viporia oscillated between excitement at new discoveries and anxiety about the rapid pace of change. Votex, while enthusiastic, sometimes got frustrated when things didn't work as he expected.

As evening approached, Frigg gathered her kittens for a final discussion. "You know, my darlings, growing up in the AI age isn't just about learning to use new technologies. It's about developing a mindset of lifelong learning."

Viporia's brow furrowed. "What do you mean, Mom?"

Frigg smiled gently. "Well, the world is changing so quickly that we need to be always ready to learn new things, to adapt, and to see challenges as opportunities for growth."

Votex yawned, the day's excitement catching up with him. "But Mom, with AI getting smarter all the time, will cats and humans still be... important in the future?"

Frigg's heart swelled with love and a touch of pride at her son's insightful question. She pulled both kittens close. "Oh, my darlings, you will always be irreplaceable. AI might be able to do many amazing things, but it will never have the curiosity, love, and spirit that you two have. Those are the things that make living creatures truly special."

As she tucked her kittens into bed that night, Frigg whispered, "Remember, my little ones, in this age of AI and technology, it's easy to get caught up in the digital world. But never forget the importance of real connections – with family, with friends, with nature. Technology is a tool, but love, kindness, and understanding are what truly make us special."

That night, as Viporia and Votex drifted off to sleep, their dreams were filled with fantastic future worlds where cats and humans worked alongside AI to solve problems and make life better for everyone. But in every dream, at the heart of every imagined future, was the warm glow of family love and the excitement of learning together.

And Frigg, as she finally managed to submit her paper (after a quick call to tech support), felt a renewed sense of purpose. She knew that guiding her kittens through this AI-filled world, with all its wonders and challenges, was her most important job of all.

Questions for Discussion:

1. According to Frigg, what is one of the most important skills for thriving in the AI age? A) Coding B) Playing video games C) Asking good questions D) Building robots Correct Answer: C

2. Why is creativity still important in the AI age? A) It isn't important anymore B) AI can't replace human creativity and emotional intelligence C) Only for making art D) To program AI Correct Answer: B

3. What did Frigg mean by a "mindset of lifelong learning"? A) Going to school forever B) Only learning about AI C) Being always ready to learn new things and adapt to changes D) Memorizing facts Correct Answer: C

4. How did Votex and Viporia react differently to learning about AI? A) They had the same reaction B) Votex was cautious, Viporia was enthusiastic C) Viporia was thoughtful and sometimes anxious, Votex was enthusiastic but occasionally frustrated D) They both disliked it Correct Answer: C

5. What did Frigg say makes living creatures special compared to AI? A) The ability to do math quickly B) Having fur C) Curiosity, love, and spirit D) The ability to use computers Correct Answer: C

Parent's Corner: Use these questions to start a conversation with your child about growing up in the AI age. You might ask:

"What kinds of questions are you curious about?" or "How do you think we can use our creativity alongside AI?" Encourage them to think about how they can develop skills that complement, rather than compete with, AI technologies.

Activity Idea: Create an "AI and Me" chart with your child. On one side, list things that AI is good at (like processing large amounts of data or recognizing patterns). On the other side, list uniquely human qualities and skills (like creativity, empathy, or asking insightful questions). Discuss how these different strengths can work together to solve problems. This activity can help children understand their own value in an AI-driven world and inspire them to develop their uniquely human qualities.

CHAPTER 9
FAMILY TIME IN A TECH WORLD

Chapter Summary for Parents: This chapter explores how to maintain strong family bonds and quality time in a world filled with technology. It covers topics such as balancing traditional and digital activities, using technology to enhance family experiences, and the importance of unplugged time. The chapter aims to provide practical ideas for families to connect meaningfully in the digital age while addressing the emotional challenges and joys of parenting in a tech-saturated world.

The gentle pitter-patter of rain against the windows created a cozy atmosphere in Frigg's home. But inside, the mood was anything but peaceful. Viporia was curled up in an armchair, her nose buried in a tablet, while Votex was sprawled on the floor, furiously tapping away at a handheld gaming device.

Frigg stood in the doorway, her whiskers twitching with a mixture of concern and frustration. She had been looking forward to a quiet family evening, but it seemed technology had other plans.

"Kittens," she called out, trying to keep the exasperation out of her voice, "don't you think we've had enough screen time for today?"

"Just five more minutes, Mom!" Votex pleaded, not even looking up from his game.

Viporia glanced up briefly, her blue eyes conflicted. "But Mom, I'm right in the middle of this really interesting article about quantum physics..."

Frigg took a deep breath, reminding herself of the delicate balance she was trying to strike between embracing technology and maintaining family connections. "I have an idea," she said, her voice brightening. "Why don't we have a family game night? We can even incorporate some tech if you'd like."

Votex's ears perked up. "Can we play that new VR game where you catch virtual fish?"

"Actually," Frigg said gently, "I was thinking we could start with a traditional board game. Then maybe we could use some tech to enhance our family time, rather than replace it."

Viporia put down her tablet, looking intrigued. "What do you mean, Mom?"

As Frigg set up an old-fashioned board game on the coffee table, she explained her idea. "We'll play this game together, face-to-face. But we can use a tablet to keep score, or even look up fun facts related to the game's theme. The key is to use technology to bring us together, not drive us apart."

Family games are always fun

As they played, giggles and playful arguments filled the room. Votex discovered he enjoyed the tactile feel of moving physical game pieces, while Viporia found herself engrossed in the strategic thinking required – something her quantum physics articles hadn't prepared her for.

Halfway through the game, Frigg introduced another activity. "Now, my darlings, let's talk about the importance of reading together as a family. In this tech world, we have more reading options than ever before."

They snuggled up on the couch as Frigg began to read from a beautifully illustrated storybook. Then they switched to an e-book on the tablet, exploring interactive features and the ability to adjust text size and brightness.

"Reading together, whether it's a paper book or an e-book, is a wonderful way to bond," Frigg explained. "It sparks imagination, builds vocabulary, and creates shared experiences. The important thing is the time we spend together, not the format of the book."

As the evening wore on, Frigg decided to address another important aspect of family time in the tech world. "Now, my curious kittens, let's talk about how we can use technology to enhance our family outings without letting it take over."

She pulled up a map on the tablet, showing nearby parks and attractions. "Technology can help us plan and discover new places to explore. We can use apps to learn about nature and history, or even play outdoor games that use our devices in creative ways."

Votex's eyes lit up. "Like a digital scavenger hunt?"

"Exactly!" Frigg beamed. "But remember, while these tech-enhanced activities can be fun, it's also important to have times when we put our devices away and simply enjoy nature and each other's company."

As bedtime approached, Frigg introduced one last topic. "Let's talk about creating and sharing digital memories," she said, picking up a digital camera.

They spent some time taking funny photos and short videos, learning how to edit them and add fun effects. Frigg showed them how to create a digital photo album, emphasizing the importance of privacy settings when sharing online.

"Creating and sharing memories is a wonderful way to bond as a family," Frigg said. "But remember, the most important thing is to be present in the moment, not just focused on capturing it for social media."

As she tucked her tired but happy kittens into bed, Viporia asked sleepily, "Mom, what's your favorite way for us to spend family time?"

Frigg's eyes sparkled with love. "My favorite moments are when we're all together, sharing, learning, and loving each other. Whether that's playing a board game, reading a story, exploring nature, or trying out a new app – what matters most is that we're doing it together."

Votex yawned, snuggling deeper into his blanket. "I liked tonight, Mom. Can we do this more often?"

Frigg purred contentedly, nuzzling each kitten in turn. "Of course, my darlings. In this tech-filled world, it's more important than ever to be intentional about our family time. Technology should bring us closer together, not drive us apart."

As Frigg turned off the light, she felt a deep sense of satisfaction. The evening hadn't gone as she'd initially planned, but it had turned into something even better – a perfect blend of traditional family time and thoughtful use of technology. She knew there would be more challenges ahead as they navigated this digital world together, but nights like these reminded her of what truly mattered.

And as Viporia and Votex drifted off to sleep, their dreams were filled with the warmth of family love, the excitement of new discoveries, and the endless possibilities of a world where technology and togetherness went hand in paw.

Questions for Discussion:

1. What was Frigg's initial concern at the beginning of the chapter? A) The rainy weather B) Her kittens spending too much time on their devices C) Not having enough technology in the house D) The kittens not doing their homework Correct Answer: B

2. How did Frigg suggest using technology during their board game night? A) To replace the board game entirely B) To keep score and look up related fun facts C) To ignore it completely D) To video call their friends Correct Answer: B

3. According to Frigg, what's important when reading together as a family? A) Only reading e-books B) Only reading paper books C) The time spent together, regardless of the book's format D) Reading as many books as possible Correct Answer: C

4. How did Frigg suggest using technology for family outings? A) To stay indoors and avoid nature B) To plan trips and enhance outdoor experiences, while also having device-free time C) To play video games in the park D) To avoid all technology during outings Correct Answer: B

5. What did Frigg say was the most important thing about creating and sharing digital memories? A) Getting the

most likes on social media B) Taking perfect photos C) Being present in the moment, not just focused on capturing it D) Buying the most expensive camera Correct Answer: C

Parent's Corner: Use these questions to start a conversation with your child about family time in the digital age. You might ask: "What's your favorite way for our family to spend time together?" or "Can you think of a way we could use technology to make our next family outing more fun or educational?" Encourage them to share their ideas about balancing tech use with family bonding.

Activity Idea: Create a "Family Tech-Time Balance Jar" with your child. Write down various family activities on small pieces of paper - some involving technology (like having a family video game tournament or creating a digital family newsletter) and some tech-free (like going for a nature walk or cooking a meal together). Each week, draw an activity from the jar to do as a family. After each activity, discuss what you enjoyed about it and how it made you feel connected as a family. This helps create a balance of tech and non-tech family time in a fun, spontaneous way while promoting reflection on the role of technology in your family life.

CHAPTER 10

LOOKING TO THE FUTURE

Chapter Summary for Parents: This final chapter explores the potential future shaped by AI and technology. It covers topics such as future careers, education, environmental solutions, and the enduring importance of human values. The chapter aims to inspire optimism and a sense of responsibility in children as they consider their role in shaping the future, while also addressing the emotional complexities of facing an uncertain yet exciting future.

The golden rays of the setting sun painted the sky in hues of orange and pink as Frigg and her kittens settled onto their favorite windowsill. Viporia and Votex gazed out at the bustling city below, their eyes wide with wonder and a hint of uncertainty.

Frigg noticed a slight tremble in Viporia's whiskers. "What's on your mind, sweetie?" she asked gently.

Viporia turned to her mother, her blue eyes filled with a mix of excitement and worry. "Mom, we've learned so much about technology, nature, and growing up in the AI age. But... what about the future? What will the world be like when we're grown up?"

Votex bounced excitedly, nearly toppling off the windowsill. "Yeah! Will we have flying cars? Or robot butlers? Or... or... space colonies for cats?"

Frigg chuckled, steadying Votex with a paw while giving Viporia a reassuring nuzzles. "The future is full of exciting possibilities, my darlings. Why don't we spend this evening imagining what the world might be like in the years to come?"

Frigg began by discussing future careers. "As technology advances, some jobs that exist today might disappear, but many new and exciting ones will be created," she explained, her eyes twinkling with enthusiasm.

"Like what?" Viporia asked, her curiosity piqued.

"Well," Frigg mused, "we might see jobs like AI Ethics Consultant, where people help ensure that artificial intelligence is used responsibly and ethically. Or how about Virtual Reality Experience Designer? They could create amazing virtual worlds for education and entertainment."

A futuristic city skyline as seen from Frigg's window.

Votex's tail swished excitedly. "Ooh, I like the sound of that! Could I design virtual fish for cats to chase?"

Frigg laughed, ruffling Votex's fur affectionately. "That's a very creative idea, Votex! And it's exactly the kind of thinking that will be valuable in the future. Jobs will likely require a mix of technical skills and creative problem-solving."

As they continued their discussion, Frigg noticed Viporia growing quieter, her brow furrowed in thought. "What's troubling you, my dear?" she asked softly.

Viporia looked up, her eyes filled with concern. "Mom, with all these changes... will we still need to learn things like reading and math? Will schools even exist?"

Frigg pulled her daughter close. "Those are very thoughtful questions, Viporia. While the methods of learning might change, the fundamental skills of reading, writing, math, and critical thinking will always be important. These basic skills help us understand and interact with the world around us, no matter how technologically advanced it becomes."

She went on to describe how education might evolve, with personalized AI tutors, virtual reality field trips, and collaborative global classrooms. But she emphasized that the human elements of teaching and learning – curiosity, creativity, and connection – would remain crucial.

As the night grew darker, Frigg decided to address a more serious topic. "Now, my curious kittens, let's talk about some of the challenges the future might bring, and how technology might help solve them."

Frigg explained concepts like renewable energy, carbon capture technology, and advanced recycling methods. "In the future," she continued, her voice filled with hope, "we might see cities powered entirely by clean energy, with smart systems that manage resources efficiently. We might have robots that clean up pollution in the oceans, or AI systems that help us predict and mitigate the effects of climate change."

Votex's eyes shone with excitement. "That's so cool! I want to build ocean-cleaning robots!"

Viporia, however, looked pensive. "But Mom, with all this amazing technology... will there still be a place for cats like us?"

Frigg's heart swelled with love and pride at her daughter's insightful question. She gathered both kittens close. "Oh, my darlings, you will always be irreplaceable. The future is full of amazing possibilities, but with all these advances comes great responsibility."

She looked each kitten in the eye. "You'll need to think carefully about how new technologies affect people, animals, and the environment. You'll need to consider questions of privacy, equality, and the balance between progress and preservation."

Viporia's whiskers twitched with determination. "So, our job is to help create a good future?"

"That's right, Viporia," Frigg purred proudly. "Each of you, in your own way, will help shape the future. Whether you become an AI designer, an environmental scientist, a teacher, or something we haven't even thought of yet, you'll have the power to make a positive difference."

As she tucked her kittens into bed, Frigg whispered, "Dream big, my little ones. Imagine all the wonderful things the future might hold. But remember, the most important things – love, kindness, curiosity, and compassion – will always be timeless."

Votex yawned, snuggling deeper into his blanket. "Even in a world with robot butlers?"

Frigg chuckled softly. "Especially in a world with robot butlers. Technology can do amazing things, but it's the warmth of family, the joy of learning, and the power of kindness that truly make life wonderful."

That night, as Viporia and Votex drifted off to sleep, their dreams were filled with visions of a bright future where technology and nature coexisted in harmony, and where their own unique talents could help make the world a better place. And at the heart of every dream was the warmth of family love and the excitement of endless possibilities.

Frigg, watching over her sleeping kittens, felt a complex mix of emotions – hope for the bright future ahead, a touch of anxiety about the challenges they might face, and an overwhelming love for these two little beings who would help shape the world to come. She knew that whatever the future held, the lessons of love, curiosity, and compassion she had shared with them would guide them well.

As she curled up beside them, Frigg purred contentedly. The future was uncertain, yes, but it was also full of promise. And she couldn't wait to see the wonderful things her kittens would do to make that future brighter for all.

Questions for Discussion

1. What example of a future career did Frigg mention? A) Flying car driver B) AI Ethics Consultant C) Robot butler programmer D) Space colony architect Correct Answer: B

2. How might education change in the future, according to Frigg? A) Schools will be eliminated entirely B) Only robots will be teachers C) There might be personalized AI tutors and virtual reality field trips D) Everyone will learn through video games Correct Answer: C

3. What did Frigg say about the importance of basic skills like reading and math in the future? A) They won't be necessary anymore B) Only math will be important C) Only reading will be important D) They will always be important, no matter how technology advances Correct Answer: D

4. What example did Frigg give of how technology might help solve environmental problems in the future? A) Building more factories B) Using more fossil fuels C) Robots cleaning up pollution in the oceans D) Cutting down all the trees Correct Answer: C

5. According to Frigg, what will always remain timeless and important in the future? A) Having the newest gadgets B) Being famous on social media C) Love, kindness, curiosity, and compassion D) Knowing how to program computers Correct Answer: C

Parent's Corner: Use these questions to start a conversation with your child about their vision for the future. You might ask: "What kind of job do you think you might like to have when you grow up?" or "If you could invent something to help the environment, what would it be?" Encourage them to think creatively and optimistically about the future while also considering their role in shaping it.

Activity Idea: Create a "Future World" collage or drawing with your child. Use magazines, drawings, or digital tools to create a visual representation of what they think the world might look like in the future. Include both technological advancements and natural elements. As you create, discuss the potential benefits and challenges of each element they include. This activity encourages creativity, critical thinking about the future, and can spark interesting discussions about progress, preservation, and the role of technology in our lives.

SUPPORT TALENT TO GROW

BRINGING YOUR STORIES TO LIGHT